Content Marketing Tutorial

The Ultimate Beginner's Guide

© 2017 COPYRIGHT

All rights reserved. No portion of this book may be reproduced in any form without permission from the publisher, except as permitted by U.S. copyright law.

DISCLAIMERS

We are not lawyers. This website and the content provided herein are simply for educational purposes and do not take the place of legal advice from your attorney. Every effort has been made to ensure that the content provided on this website is accurate and helpful for our readers at publishing time. However, this is not an exhaustive treatment of the subjects. No liability is assumed for losses or damages due to the information provided. You are responsible for your own choices, actions, and results. You should consult your attorney for your specific publishing and disclaimer questions and needs.

This is a work of fiction. Names, characters, places, and incidents either are the products of the author's imagination or are used fictitiously. Any resemblance to actual persons, living or dead, businesses, companies, events, or locales is entirely coincidental.

Content Marketing Tutorial

Content Marketing is all about creating and distributing content that engages and attracts a targeted audience, while encouraging them to take action which is profitable to a business. This is a brief tutorial that explains how you can use content marketing to your advantage and promote your business.

Audience

This tutorial is primarily going to help all those readers who are into advertising and specifically those who aspire to make a career in Digital Marketing.

Prerequisites

Before proceeding with this tutorial, you should have a good understanding of the fundamental concepts of marketing, advertising, and analyzing products and audience.

Contents

Content Marketing Tutorial 1
The Ultimate Beginner's Guide 1
© 2017 COPYRIGHT 2
DISCLAIMERS 3
Content Marketing Tutorial 4
Audience 5
Prerequisites 6
What is Content Marketing? 8
What is the Use of Content Marketing? 9
Content Marketing Strategy 10
Identify & Understand the Customer 11
List Your Primary Customers 11
Collect Information about Your Customers 11
Identify the Characteristics of Your Primary Customers 12
Create Personas 12
Story Building & Content Creation 14
Why are You Creating the Content? 15
Who are Your Customers? 15
What do You Want Your Content to Archive? 16
Content Marketing Media Channels 17
Analysis of Your Situation 17
Your Channel Objectives 17
Content Plan for Your Channel 18
Editorial Calendar & Style Guides 19
What is an Editorial Calendar? 19

How to Build an Editorial Calendar 19
What is a Style Guide? 21
Content Marketing Tools 21
Content Creation and Publishing Tools 23
Conversion and Data Capture Tools..23
Content Optimization Tools 23
Social Media Management and Listening Tools 24
Challenges & Solutions 24
Research, Research, and Research..25
Resist Content Overkill 26
Define Your Content Budget 26
Measuring & Tracking Success...27
Measuring and Tracking Sales..27
Measuring and Tracking Cost Savings 28
Measuring and Tracking Customer Retention...28
Content Marketing Blogs 30
What is Blog? 30
How a Blog Works 31
Benefits of Maintaining a Blog 32
Lifecycle Emails & eNewsletters 33
What are Lifecycle Emails and eNewsletters? 33
How do Lifecycle Emails Work? 34
How do eNewsletters Work? 35
Benefits of Using Lifecycle Emails and eNewsletters..................................36
WhitePapers & Case Studies...37
What is a Whitepaper?...37

Purpose of Writing a Whitepaper 37
What is a Case Study? 39
Purpose of Writing a Case Study 39
eBooks & Digital Magazines 40
What is an eBook? 40
Benefits of Using eBooks 40
What is a Digital Magazine? 40
Benefits of Using Digital Magazines 41
Mobile & Web-Based Applications 42
What are Mobile and Web-based Applications? 42
How to Use Mobile Apps for Content Marketing 43
How to Use Web Applications for Content Marketing 43
Podcasts & Webinars 45
What are Podcasts and Webinars? 45
Tips to create a successful Podcast 46
Tips to create a successful Webinar 47
Benefits of Using Podcasts 47
Benefits of Using Webinars 49
Videos & Infographics 49
What are Infographics? 49
Tips to Create a Good Infographic 51
Benefits of Using Infographics 52
Articles & Press Releases 53
What are Articles and Press Releases? 53
How to Use Articles 53
How to Use Press Releases 54

Benefits of Using Articles and Press Releases 54

Social Media Channels 55

How to Use Social Media Channels 55

Facebook & Twitter 55

Youtube & Vimeo 57

Instagram & Flickr 58

Pinterest & Quora 59

Benefits of Using Social Media Channels 60

Content Marketing Examples 61

Ford 61

Lauren Lake 61

Baby Center 61

Web Resources 62

Content Marketing Institute 63

MOZ 63

Copyblogger 63

QuickSprout 63

What is Content Marketing?

Content marketing is known by many names such as inbound marketing, corporate journalism, branded media, native advertising, and customer publishing to name a few. However, the basic idea behind the strategy remains the same, i.e., to create and distribute content that engages and attracts a targeted audience, while encouraging them to take action which is profitable to a business.

What is the Use of Content Marketing?

The growth of the World Wide Web, social networks, and mobile technologies has changed the relationship between consumers and businesses. Average consumers today don't buy a product just by passively watching its advertisement on a billboard. They research on Google to compare similar products, read the product's review online by experts, and even ask their friends on social networks, before spending their money.

As a result, businesses need to rethink their traditional marketing strategies and channels if they want to earn the trust of their customers and influence their buying decisions. This is where content marketing plays an important role. It helps businesses to attract potential consumers' attention towards their products by highlighting and promoting their key features.

Content Marketing Strategy

Before you create a content marketing strategy for your business, you need to define the goals first. What are you trying to achieve with your content? Is it more subscribers to your blog? Or is it traffic acquisition? Or maybe, you want certain sales pages of your website to convert? Whatever they are, you need to clearly list the goals before you even begin laying down the strategy.

That being said, there are certain overarching elements to a content marketing strategy which are the same, regardless of your goals. They are listed in brief below, as we will look into them in detail later in this tutorial:

- Understanding your customers

- Building your brand message or story

- Defining the content you want to create

- Measuring the success of your content marketing efforts

Identify & Understand the Customer

Identifying your target audience is the easy part. What is more challenging for a business is to understand the pain points of its customers. Once you grasp the problems of your consumers and understand their requirements, you would be able to come up with perfect solutions to cater to those particular requirements.

When you want to create a content marketing strategy, finding out about your audiences and their needs is the most important task. But how do you make sure that you have penned down the real problems of your customers and not just imagined them? You can do this by following the four steps mentioned below:

List Your Primary Customers

To accurately list your primary customers, give them specific names and identities. For instance, if you run a travel company, your audiences might fall under: experienced travelers, occasional travelers, tourists visiting a city, local residents touring the city, etc.

Collect Information about Your Customers

You can collect information about your major customers in a number of ways such as:

- Conduct a survey of customers visiting your site

- Ask your customer service for the questions customers are asking

- Read the emails and feedback of customers on your Contact or Help page

Identify the Characteristics of Your Primary Customers

Identifying the characteristics of your primary customers means learning about your customers' experiences. For example, experienced travelers might know about airport codes and e-tickets but occasional travelers might not. Such well-rounded information helps you to build content that caters to each and every customer's needs.

Create Personas

The best way to visualize and understand a customer's needs is to create personas. While creating personas, give specific details to a customer, for instance:

- Assign a name - John

- Age - 45 years old

- Profession - Senior IT manager

- Web tasks - Reads technology news daily, books travel tickets, buys things on weekends, etc.

Story Building & Content Creation

Marketing gurus and pundits have often repeated the line that it's the company that tells a better story wins and not the company which is bigger in size. This truism is even more relevant today with the growth of new forms of online media, which have empowered consumers like never before.

However, the question still remains largely unanswered. How do you tell a better story? Do you create a 10x10 feet poster, listing out the features of your product, and stick it on every billboard in town or do you create a swanky television advertisement? Which is the option that will give you more business and more revenue? Well, to be honest, building a good story and creating great content requires much more than that. It requires you to answer the 3Ws: **who, what,** and **why**.

To create a great story around your business, you need to clearly answer the following:

Why are You Creating the Content?

Defining your content goals is the first step.

- Why do you want to create a specific type of content?
- What is it that you want to accomplish?
- Does the content strategy match your overall business goals?

These are important questions that need to be answered.

Who are Your Customers?

It goes without saying that identifying your customers is the most important step of content marketing. You can refer to Part 2 of this tutorial to learn how to identify your customers. The bottom line is to list out the problems and preferences of your audience and figure out what kinds of content will they like best. Also, you need to answer the important question - **what is the unique thing that you have to offer to you customers?**

What do You Want Your Content to Archive?

You must ask yourself - how will my content help my customers? Will it help them to arrange a travel, buy a house, or train for an examination? You need to clearly define and understand how your content will affect the lives of your customers?

Content Marketing Media Channels

By media channels, we mean the platform you decide to use in order to market your content. This is an important step of your overall content marketing strategy because the channel also determines what content you must create. For instance, if the channel is a blog, then the content you can create are feature stories, product announcements, etc. Similarly, if it's your website's Facebook Page, then the content can be images, status messages, weblinks, etc.

There are three major strategies that you must consider while defining your media channels:

Analysis of Your Situation

The first thing to do is to understand what existing channels do you have and which new ones you need or want.

- Do you already have a Facebook Page for your website?
- Do you need to develop a separate blog?
- Will it help in telling your story effectively to your customers?

The information about your customers and the story you want to tell are both crucial in deciding what media channels you want. It also depends on your budget and bandwidth.

Your Channel Objectives

Now that you have a fair idea of your situation, you need to map the objectives of your channels. For instance, depending on the story you want to tell and your content marketing goals, you might decide that a blog would be the best channel. So your channel's primary objective would be to get more subscribers to your blog, which will generate leads for your sales.

Content Plan for Your Channel

This is the part where you bring together your channel objectives and your content plan. Taking the above example, the primary objective of your blog is to get more subscribers, which brings in more leads. To achieve this, you might decide to write a couple of articles and club them together as an ebook, which you can then provide for free to new subscribers. However, before you decide the right content for your channel, you also need to consider the different personas of your customers.

Editorial Calendar & Style Guides

What is an Editorial Calendar?

Content marketing is a long-term strategy and an editorial calendar helps you plan your strategy in an organized fashion. The calendar will contain details such as:

- List of the kinds of content you have or need to create, including the dates when they will be created and published
- The names of the content editors/producers and other stakeholders who are responsible for the project
- The media channel that you will use to market your content
- Metadata such as your primary target audience, SEO keywords, call to action, etc.

How to Build an Editorial Calendar

While you can use a simple tool such as an Excel or Google sheet to create an editorial calendar, you can also use web-based software offered by companies such as HubSpot, Skyword, etc.

What is a Style Guide?

A content marketing style guide is a document which standardizes your content creation guidelines. From the colors of your brand, the key phrases you use for call to action buttons to the spelling and punctuation usages, everything is documented and standardized by a style guide.

A style guide is a necessary document for the success of your content marketing strategy as well as to maintain quality of the content across your website. A style guide can list step-by-step rules for:

- **A designer's checklist** - This will remind designers of your brand colors, correct image properties and copyright issues, icon selection, etc.

- **A writer's checklist** - This will remind writers of the use of voice, spelling, punctuation, unique words, and phrases approved by the company. It will also advise writes on legal fact checking and proofreading methods.

Content Marketing Tools

Content Marketing tools come in different shapes and sizes. What will work for you is totally dependent on your business requirements and the scope of your content marketing strategy. The tools listed below cover the three central aspects of content creation, management, and optimization.

Content Creation and Publishing Tools

These tools will help you create a website from scratch, build your blog, and send emails to your subscribers and publish almost any kind of content. Known as content management tools, these range from the simple and free ones such as **Wordpress** and **Drupal** to the paid ones such as **Sitecore** and **Tridion**.

Conversion and Data Capture Tools

What these tools do is allow you to build online registration forms and surveys for your key landing pages. They capture data of customers visiting these landing pages, which can be integrated with sales tools like Salesforce.com. Examples include Wufoo, Equola, Manticore, etc.

Content Optimization Tools

These are tools that help you to deliver specific content to targeted customers. Once users come to your website and identify themselves, these tools push content which are relevant to these users.

For instance, let's say you own a travel website and a user comes and identifies himself as a tourist looking for cars in the city, now these tools will filter your content and provide the user only the relevant information, while hiding the irrelevant ones. Examples of such tools include Google Website Optimizer, Adobe Omniture, Autonomy Optimost, etc.

Social Media Management and Listening Tools

These tools are excellent for managing and tracking the content for your social channels such as Facebook ad Twitter. One of the most frequently used tools is **Hootsuite**, which allows you to centrally schedule your social media posts. For Twitter, you can use **Tweetdeck** and for further analysis, you can grab tools like **Radian6** and **Sysomos**.

Challenges & Solutions

Developing the perfect content marketing strategy for your business is not easy. You have to accurately identify your target customers and understand their problems. You have to define your media channels and build editorial style guides. You have to make sure that your story will resonate with your audience without misleading them.

However, even after you've managed to bring all the pieces of your strategy together, three crucial challenges still remain:

- Creating engaging content

- Creating enough content

- Finding the budget to create the content

Let's look at some of the ways in which you can solve these problems:

Research, Research, and Research

The first rule of creating engaging content that's right for your audience is by way of research.

- Don't assume that you know exactly what kind of content your customers will like or need.

- Do some market research to find out what your competitors are doing.

- Gather feedback from your customers.

- Look at data and analytics of your website's traffic.

- Test your webpages and email campaigns.

The bottom line is to not regard yourself as an expert but a learner of the art of content marketing.

Resist Content Overkill

As in life, where you will not always make the correct decisions; not every content piece you create will do well either. Your webpages might see fantastic traffic but your blog might not be getting as many subscribers as you hoped it would.

- Don't panic and start spamming your blog with one article after another.

- Instead, spend time on producing quality content that is a clear reflection of your brand message and story.

The trick is not to produce a ton of random content but well-researched content that will offer lasting value to your customers.

Define Your Content Budget

Once you understand what kinds of content you will create, find out how much of it is **one-time content** such as a webpage and how much of it is **ongoing content** such as blog articles.

This will give you a fair idea of how much you need to spend on creating content. Then you can decide whether you want to build an in-house content team or want to rope in freelancers. However, make sure you hire the right persons. For instance, someone with a journalistic background will be able to write you the best blogposts, while a copywriter will pen down the perfect call to action content for your webpages.

Measuring & Tracking Success

Whether you're creating a content marketing strategy for your own business or a client, the primary questions still remains - What's the Return on Investment (ROI)? For all the efforts you've put in your content marketing strategy, the ROI needs to be positive.

What constitutes ROI varies from business to business. However, every successful content marketing strategy needs to answer at least one of the three crucial questions listed below:

- Has it driven sales for the business?
- Has it saved costs for the company?
- Has it helped in making customers lives easier, thus increasing retention?

To sum it up, a growth in sales, decrease in costs, and customer retention are the three key areas which determine the success of a content marketing strategy. Let's look at each of these points in more detail:

Measuring and Tracking Sales

Measuring and tracking sales is the part which answers whether your business actually made any money. The results of your content marketing strategy must need to answer questions such as:

- Did you make any sales through your e-commerce section?
- How many visitors came though organic or inorganic search and bought your product or service?

You can measure all of this by looking at you sales metrics in your own CRM and Google analytics.

Measuring and Tracking Cost Savings

Cost savings is basically your actual profit: (Converted Leads – Total Cost per Lead). While calculating the total costs per lead, you need to factor in the money you spent paying employees or freelancers in creating the content for you. This also includes all the overheads such as the rent, insurance, utilities, design costs, hosting fees, subscriptions, and software costs.

Measuring and Tracking Customer Retention

By customer retention, we not only mean the new leads coming in but also the average life of the existing customers. Your goals must be to keep all customers longer and happier. You can measure this via your CRM to track what kinds of content are being consumed by your customers and measure whether that content has helped in retention and renewal of subscriptions.

Content Marketing Blogs

What is Blog?

A blog is an excellent tool for creating and publishing content. It can be your website's home base or a hub for your content, where you can write posts such as product announcements, service guides, thought leadership articles, press announcements, and more. It is basically a platform for you to share your ideas and thoughts with the world.

How a Blog Works

There are certain basic rules that you need to follow, especially if you are writing a business blog:

- Know your audience and keep in mind the goals you're trying to achieve through your blog. Track if these goals are being met via Google or your custom analytics tool.
- Write down killer headlines which will improve the open-rate of your blogposts, especially if you are marketing it via Enewsletters or life-cycle emails.
- Design your blog so that it not only looks beautiful but helps your customers to easily find items such as the RSS subscription icon, a search box, your contact information, and social sharing icons.
- Make sure that you have categorized your topics well. Add relevant keywords and tags to your topics so that customers can easily find the blogposts.
- Keep an eye out for spam comments and enable the comment moderation feature which allows you to filter spams.

Benefits of Maintaining a Blog

A blog is primarily a community-building tool, a place for generating leads based on new subscriptions, which might also directly or indirectly lead to a sale. It is also an excellent tool for content maximization, for instance, let's say you have created a new video tutorial for your customers, which you've published on your website and on YouTube. Now, you create a blogpost for the same and market this video on your blog. Most importantly, your blog helps to nurture good relations with your customers and retain them longer.

Lifecycle Emails & eNewsletters

What are Lifecycle Emails and eNewsletters?

Lifecycle emails and eNewsletters are basically permission-based emails that offer value to your customers. When your customers sign-up for your product or service, you can prompt them for these email subscriptions.

While eNewsletters are typically distributed weekly or monthly, the distribution of lifecycle emails can vary according to your campaign. Let's look at when and why you can send these emails.

How do Lifecycle Emails Work?

These are emails with educational content in them for new customers. By educational content, we mean certain insights, strategies, or know-how's that you as a business offer to your customers in order help them with their tasks.

For instance, let's say you are an eLearning company which sells training software to companies. You can create lifecycle emails, which provide your customers with helpful strategies in overcoming training-related challenges such as reducing costs and saving employee work-hours. You can spread these life-cycle emails over the course of a week, month, or even a year.

How do eNewsletters Work?

eNewsletters are emails you send out to both existing and new customers. The emails can contain information about your product, service, or even company-related information. You can include full-length articles or short image-based content, which links out to some specific landing pages of your website.

Benefits of Using Lifecycle Emails and eNewsletters

The benefits of circulating lifecycle emails and enewsletters are manifold. Since lifecycle emails are targeted for your new customers, their primary goal is to drive your sales funnel. However, you are not directly pitching your customers a product or a service. Instead, you are trying to offer them value, so that they look at you as thought leaders in the industry. In that sense, it is more of brand building but one that gently pushes your customers towards a sale.

An eNewsletters is a promotional tool for your content. For instance, you can email your customers a new whitepaper, an ebook, a webinar, or a video that you have recently created. You can also create aggregated content such as a round-up of all your blogposts for a particular month and send it out as an eNewsletters to your customers.

WhitePapers & Case Studies

Both whitepapers and case studies are primarily B2B marketing content, however there is a thin line of difference in the way they work.

What is a Whitepaper?

A whitepaper, also called a **research paper**, is a kind of an extended report which focuses on a particular topic, elaborates it, and explains it in detail.

- A whitepaper is a long and linear narrative which argues a certain concept, while backing the argument with data and research.

- The language used in a whitepaper is formal, which might also include technical jargon used by experts.

- A whitepaper can consist of statistical tables, quotes from leading research firms, excerpts from academic books, etc.

- The contents of a whitepaper should be text-heavy meant for deep reading.

Purpose of Writing a Whitepaper

With a whitepaper, you can talk about your expertise and educate prospective customers about your business. If you sell a product or provide a service, which customers buy or subscribe to only after due research, then you can come up with a whitepaper which guides them in their buying decisions.

What is a Case Study?

Case studies feature a client story, narrating how a client used your product or service to achieve its business goals.

- A case study is typically a first-person narrative written in the form of a story.
- It is a testimonial which relates a real-life event.
- It is written in a simple format telling readers about a certain company's challenges, solutions and results, at times using direct quotes from the company.

Purpose of Writing a Case Study

A case study is basically trust-building content. It is created with the intent to build your credibility and trust among your customers by sharing a real-life story. For instance, If your company sells training software and solutions to other companies, then a possible case study might feature how a certain company used your tools to bring down its training costs and save time. You can market this case study as a press announcement, email campaign, and even host this content on a particular landing page of your website.

eBooks & Digital Magazines

What is an eBook?

An ebook is like a whitepaper but it is more informal, loose, and more playful. The language used is more everyday talk and is designed in a visual manner. The content must be entertaining and easily consumable with bold headlines, callouts, and bulleted lists.

- An ebook is written in a very concise style keeping in mind that readers skim and skip.

- The content is highly-visual and the ideas and concepts an ebook contains have to be interesting and preferably those that are trending and current.

Benefits of Using eBooks

Ebooks are awesome because they can bring your website traffic and generate more leads. You can market free ebooks, as an incentive for new customers to subscribe. When they land on a specific page of your website, you can prompt them to collect their free ebook. You can also market these ebooks via email campaigns. However, make sure that you add clear call to action buttons in your ebooks so that readers are directed to your key pages.

What is a Digital Magazine?

A digital magazine is a periodical, which is something in between a PDF and a traditional magazine. It can be a fortnightly or monthly magazine containing a variety of content from articles, videos, podcasts, and more.

A digital magazine is an awesome tool for presenting a ton of content that you already have but don't want to host on your main website. For instance, you can create a digital magazine consisting of infographics, podcasts, videos, etc. You might not want this content to be an integral part of your website, but you still want them as they serve a specific purpose such as capturing long-tail SEO keywords that your website's content doesn't.

Benefits of Using Digital Magazines

Digital magazines can become a great hub for your content. For instance, you can create content around certain keywords and host them in your digital magazine. It is also an excellent platform for integrating all your offline content such as brochures, books, etc. and giving them an online presence.

Mobile & Web-Based Applications

What are Mobile and Web-based Applications?

Mobile as well as web-based applications are awesome tools for marketing your content to a populace, which is increasingly using their smartphones instead of their PCs to access the Internet. Though mobile apps are in the trend, you should not limit yourself to these. You should also create web-based applications, which are built to serve a specific use and customer base; and can be accessed from desktops, laptops, and even mobiles.

How to Use Mobile Apps for Content Marketing

If your business is about selling a service or a product online, then you should definitely consider creating a mobile application as one of your priority content goals. You can create a native app built for specific platforms and devices such as Android, iPhone, iPad, Blackberry, and more.

One of the reasons why you should create mobile applications as part of your content marketing strategy is because today most people access the internet from their smartphones rather than their PCs. Having a mobile application for your business helps you capture this customer segment and drive more traffic and sales.

How to Use Web Applications for Content Marketing

You can create web-based applications that are mobile responsive and market them on specific marketplaces such as Chrome Web Store. You can also host these web-based applications on your website to help your customers tackle a problem or complete a task. For instance, let's assume your company sells insurance policies. You could create a custom application such as a tax calculator, which will calculate the tax savings of users who want to take a certain policy. Customers can download these applications and use them when they want, with or without an internet connection.

You need to develop a web-based application if it helps your customers complete a task they perform on a daily basis. Web-based applications bring in new customers onboard as they sign-up or download these applications. It also helps in retaining existing customers, while positioning you as a thought leader in the industry.

Podcasts & Webinars

What are Podcasts and Webinars?

Podcast and webinars are spectacular pieces of content that can be easily consumed, by an audience, without any hassles. Unlike an online video, customers can listen to your podcast or webinar anytime, whether they're driving or jogging. That being said, both podcasts and webinars can use videos. However, audio podcasts are more popular and preferred by most people, while a webinar typically is accompanied by online presentations.

A podcast is primarily a one-way communication, where you pre-record a discussion on a topic that will interest your customers, and then release it for your audience.

A webinar goes a bit further, as it is a participatory experience, where attendees can access the conference via a weblink or a meeting invitation.

Tips to create a successful Podcast

- You can create a podcast out of your existing videos such as those with a presentation or speech. Simply remove the visuals and capture only the audio.
- Research on what kind of podcast you want to create. Listen to some podcasts and see if you like the casual and conversation style or the more formal business meeting kind of talk show.
- Keep your podcasts short enough to be engaging and long enough to be useful. A 30-minute podcast is pretty much the standard.
- Do not forget to plan and make notes of what topics and things you will be discussing in your podcast. This helps you to stay focused and not stray from the main topic.
- You can also add music to the opening and closing of your podcast but always use licensed music, as you don't want any lawsuits.

Tips to create a successful Webinar

- Research the problems your customers are facing and always tackle these issues in your webinars.
- Your webinar can be a **how-to** content which offers specific steps and information or thought provoking and strategic content. Decide which one works best for your customers.
- Create a storyboard where you have the structure of your webinar fully laid out. This helps you to progress logically and step by step through the webinar without confusing participants.
- Create really catchy titles such as "Top 5 Essential Strategies for Creating a Killer Facebook Page."

Benefits of Using Podcasts

- A podcast is a great tool to talk to your target audience and can be a great community-building tool.
- You can distribute the podcasts as an RSS feed on your website or on podcast directories such as iTunes.

- The best thing about podcasts is that you can take any existing content that you have such as a presentation, video, or even a blogpost and then re-hash it to create a script for your podcast.

Benefits of Using Webinars

- Webinars, or **webcasts** as they are alternatively called, are very effective for B2B content marketing.

- Webinars are primarily looked upon as educational content and helps you to set yourself as a thought leader in the business.

- By offering quick and actionable tips that resonate with your audience, you can earn their trust and word-of-mouth recommendation.

Videos & Infographics

What are Infographics?

Almost every business today creates a video or infographics as part of their content marketing program. In a business context, you can use videos to give customers a guided tour of your product or service. With infographics, you can help your customers understand a specific problem that you solve for them.

However, the use of videos and infographics are not limited to product tutorials and guides. With the unprecedented growth of video sites like YouTube and Vimeo and infographic sites like Listly, you can use videos and infographics to create brand awareness, generate sales leads and establish yourself as a thought leader in the industry.

Tips to Create a Good Infographic

Contrary to popular belief, it is not an expensive affair to create a decent video or an infographic. However, the focus must not be solely on creating content that goes viral but content that tells a story that your customers will find interesting.

- Even if it's about your product or service, it doesn't have to be overtly serious. Create video or infographics that entertain, while at the same time, educate your customers.
- List out what your video or infographic will feature. Will it tell a real story of only your company or include your clients, vendors, customers, etc.?
- In the case of a video, the first part is to create an excellent script. The second part includes the voice-over and visuals. Hire professionals to do these jobs for you.
- Though many infographics include data and statistics, a great infographic has to do much more. That is, it has to provide insights into the data and show how all the information adds up.

Benefits of Using Infographics

To say that videos and infographics are a great addition to your content marketing strategy would be an understatement. They are very essential, as they have massive reach, owing to their visual nature and potential to go viral.

Since Google today has a blended search approach, your videos and infographics can improve your Google rankings and bring in more traffic to your website.

Articles & Press Releases

What are Articles and Press Releases?

Whether they be the good old long-copy feature articles or the new-fangled, instruction based, step-by-step how-to ones, articles are essential to the success of your content marketing strategy. You can use articles to

- Discuss industry trends
- Offer solutions to typical concerns of customers
- start a discussion

Similarly, press releases or **online new releases** as they are often called, are essential to provide your brand more exposure and recognition. Generally a press release comes under PR and marketing, and they help you to inform your potential buyers of your products and services.

How to Use Articles

Creating articles is the best way for your business to directly address the concerns of your audience. However, creating a single article is not going to help. You need to create an article campaign for which you need to include your SEO team and create a keyword campaign. Based on this and other accompanying research such as competitor and market analysis, you can create well-informed articles, which speak to your readers.

How to Use Press Releases

For press releases, you need to have a story to tell. Refer to **Story Building and Content Creation** to learn how to build a great story around your business. It doesn't matter if you don't have a new per say such as new product launch or service expansion, what you must be able to tell is a really good story with your press release.

Benefits of Using Articles and Press Releases

Though it is regarded that online readers do not like reading long copy, however, creating high quality articles and publishing them in top tier sites like Washington Post, Mashable, Huffington Post can drive huge traffic to your website and grow your list of subscribers and sales leads. Again, publishing thought-leadership pieces on your community blog can attract potential customers as well as people who can influence your customers buying decisions such as industry experts.

What a press release does for you is pretty much straightforward – inform potential customers about your product or service and induce them to buy or subscribe.

Social Media Channels

How to Use Social Media Channels

Social media promotion has become an **esse**ntial part of any content marketing strategy today. This includes B2B and B2C marketing aspects and covers different social media channels such as social sharing networks, video channels, photo sharing sites, online communities, and more.

Among the different social media channels, some of the most popular ones are Facebook, Twitter, Youtube, Vimeo, Instagram, Flickr, Pinterest, and Quora. However, they are all similar yet different from each other. Let's look at them in more detail.

Facebook & Twitter

Facebook and Twitter are the prime social network channels. Facebook, with more than a billion users, is used by most, if not all, of your customers. Twitter is another tool that is equally effective when it comes to reaching out to your customers. That being said, let's look at how you can optimize these channels:

- Share interesting but brief content such as compelling messages or shareable pictures.

- Consider posting contests and giveaways.

- Use hashtags generously but always be relevant to the context.

- Cover industry events, well-edited images, interesting quotes, and whatever you think works with your audience.

Youtube & Vimeo

Youtube and Vimeo are video channels where you can store your videos online and allow people to embed them on their websites and blogs. Let's look at how you can optimize your business using these channels:

- Always allow embedding of your videos as you want as many people to share them as possible.

- Create short videos and unlike a 10 minute long-drawn story, show snippets of scenes stitched together in a 1 to 2 minute video.

- Make videos about customers and their problems, not about your company.

Instagram & Flickr

Instagram and Flickr are the most prominent photo sharing sites on the internet. Let's look at how you can use these channels to market your content:

- Drive back traffic to your website by linking relevant call to action button in your images and photos.

- Try sharing not only official content but photos that bring out your brand's personality. A kind of 'behind the scenes' image of your company.

- Build a strong community by asking your followers to post photos for a contest.

Pinterest & Quora

Pinterest and Quora are basically online communities and among the largest today. Let's look at how you can utilize these channels:

- With Pinterest, don't just post images and pictures. You can even pin videos and landing pages, so that customers are encouraged to interact with your website's actual content.

- As for Quroa, it's all about asking the right questions and answering them correctly. You should also follow topics and people who can influence your customers to buy your product or service.

Benefits of Using Social Media Channels

The explosion of social media in the last decade has changed the way we interact with each other online. This has also changed the way businesses communicate with their customers. As a result, social media marketing helps your business in many ways such as:

- Build you brand reputation and recognition among potential buyers.

- Drive traffic to your websites, which can lead to sales.

- Gives small-to-medium size businesses a level playing field, where they can still get customers even if they do not rank in search engines.

- Allows you to directly interact with customers and understand their problems better.

Content Marketing Examples

While there could be a thousand best examples of content marketing, we'll discuss here three brands, who are creating the most compelling content, ideas, and strategies.

Ford

This has to be one of the smartest community building campaigns by any company so far. It is a platform for Ford customers to share their ideas and stories with Ford. Ford uses all kinds of content – articles, photos, videos – to tell their story, while never failing to make it all about the customer.

Lauren Lake

Lauren Luke was a make-up artist who struck gold with her video tutorials on YouTube – which collectively have over 135 million views and 500,000+ subscribers. She has built a bigger brand out of YouTube than many top cosmetic companies on YouTube, all because of her DIY makeup video tutorials.

Baby Center

Baby Center is hands down the most educational website ever. It has a ton of information-based articles, all of which are very well written and relevant to people who are planning for a baby or are learning to become parents. This website is a stellar example of how to create highly informational articles to address the problems of your audiences.

Web Resources

There are plenty of web resources out there, but here we will highlight the top four resources for learning content marketing in a holistic manner. Since content marketing includes the whole gamut from content creation, search engine optimization and data analysis, the resources included here also have specialization in one or two of these areas.

Content Marketing Institute

Joe Pulizzi is the enigmatic founder of CMI - the most relevant and important online resource for learning what content marketing is and how to use it for your business. You can listen to podcasts, register for a webinar, read articles and its monthly magazine, or even take an online course with CMI to learn everything there's to know about content marketing.

MOZ

This is a website that every search engine marketer needs to refer to, at least three times a day. It is a place to learn search engine marketing and its related aspects such as link building, Google Algorithm, on-page optimization, social media strategies, and a lot more. Additionally, it offers excellent tools like Open Site Explorer and MozBar that help you to measure and track your content marketing success.

Copyblogger

A godsend for content writers and editors, this is the ultimate website when it comes to finding the most useful tips and strategies on creating content that engages and sells. From writing the best copy for your landing pages, coming up with crisp titles for your blogposts, to creating killer video scripts; you will find the most helpful tips on anything and everything concerning content marketing and copywriting here.

QuickSprout

QuickSprout is a well-known blog owned and run by Neil Patel, whom Forbes hails as one of the top ten online marketers in the world. His blog is a must read for all content marketers, as it gives handy tips on different aspects of online marketing. What makes it special is its data-driven approach, where Neil backs up his examples with data and analysis. This is a good place to learn how data synergizes with your content marketing efforts.

www.ingramcontent.com/pod-product-compliance
Lightning Source LLC
Chambersburg PA
CBHW050018230526
45470CB00003B/1029